THE HARD WORK OF
REST

BUILDING BLOCKS FOR
Life@Work®

WORD PUBLISHING

NASHVILLE

A Thomas Nelson Company

™Life@Work Co.®

Published by Word Publishing, a division of Thomas Nelson Company, P. O. Box 141000, Nashville, Tennessee, 37214, in association with the literary agency of Alive Communications, Inc., 7680 Goddard Street, Suite 200, Colorado Springs, Colorado, 80920.

Unless otherwise indicated, Scripture quotations used in this book are from The Holy Bible, New International Version (NIV). Copyright ©1973, 1978, 1984, International Bible Society. Used by permission of Zondervan Bible Publishers.

ISBN 0-8499-4261-6

Printed in the United States of America
0 1 2 3 4 PHX 9 8 7 6 5 4 3 2 1

INTRODUCTION

It's common for followers of Christ to struggle when trying to integrate their faith with their work lives. Unfortunately, there is not much support for Christ-centered values in the business world. That's why we put together this Building Blocks series.

The Life@Work team drilled into five core topics essential for a strong foundation of Biblical values: ambition, calling, ethics, rest, and mentoring. Knowing that you have a limited amount of time, we extracted sixteen key principles and intentionally made them a quick read. Yet, each principle contains an essential piece of the puzzle. When you integrate these principles into the big picture of your work life, we believe you will walk in greater freedom and security as a child of God.

This fourth book in the series addresses the many elements of rest. What does rest have to do with work? Aren't they opposite ends of the same spectrum? How do we tell the difference between needing rest and just being lazy? Scripture and the experience of seasoned leaders in the business world have a lot to say about these and other issues regarding the value of rest.

As the founding partners of The Life@Work Co.®, the integration of faith and work is our collective life missions, and these books are the by-products of years of study and interviews with practitioners.

The Building Blocks series was written in collaboration with Stephen Caldwell, executive editor of *The Life@Work Journal,* and Bob Tamasy, publications director for CBMC International and a frequent contributor to *Life@Work.* We hope these books help you find satisfaction and success from a well-invested life at work!

Stephen Graves
Thomas Addington
Sean Womack

THE HARD WORK OF

REST

The Sabbath is not for the sake of weekdays; the weekdays are for the sake of Sabbath. It is not an interlude but the climax of living.

—Abraham Joshua Heschel

PRINCIPLE ONE

Rest is part of the rythm of life:
a mandate from God.

While at Princeton Seminary, Edwin R. Roberts reportedly sat under a pastor who vowed not to take vacations. After all, he said, "the devil never does." After doing some research on the matter, Roberts could not help but wonder: Whose example are we to follow? The devil's, or God's?

Rest is so important to God that He not only took a break after the work of creation, but He also made rest a requirement for those who want to be close to Him. He blessed the seventh day—the day that He rested—and He made it holy (Genesis 2:2–3).

Philo, a spokesman of the Greek-speaking Jews of Alexandria during the Roman rule over Israel, defended the practice of the Sabbath in the spirit of Aristotle—by explaining that rest makes man more productive. According to Jewish writer Abraham Joshua Heschel, Philo explained it this way: "On this day we are commanded to abstain from all work, not because the law inculcates slackness. . . . Its object is rather to give man relaxation from continuous and unending toil and by refreshing their bodies with a regularly calculated system of remissions and send them out renewed to their old activities. For a breathing spell enables not merely ordinary people but athletes also to collect their strength with a stronger force behind them to undertake promptly and patiently each of the tasks set before them."

But as Heschel points out in *The Sabbath: Its Meaning for Modern Man*, the Sabbath is much more than a time to recharge the battery. "To observe the Sabbath," he writes, "is to celebrate the coronation of a day in the spiritual wonderland of time, the air of which we inhale when we 'call it a delight.'"[1]

In addition to the practice of the Sabbath, the Bible is filled with illustrations of the value of rest—taking a day off to celebrate God's creation, leaving a field fallow, breaking for prayer, fasting. Rest, in God's eyes, is part of the rhythm of life, the refreshing pause that gives renewed strength to the athlete or adds beauty to a musical score.

Jesus not only kept the Sabbath, but He also made rest a priority and encouraged His disciples to do the same. When the disciples returned from their first mission trip and everyone was wound up and excited, Jesus said, "Come with me by yourselves to a quiet place and get some rest" (Mark 6:31). At the key times during His ministry, in fact, Jesus didn't work harder—He retreated to a solitary place for rest. Roberts, in fact, discovered that the Gospels mention ten periods of retirement during the three years of Jesus' active ministry, not including nightly rest and Sabbath rest.

"His was a life of beautiful balance," Chuck Swindoll wrote in *Leisure: Having Fun Is Serious Business*. "He accomplished everything the Father sent Him to do. Everything. And He did it without ignoring those essential times of leisure. If that is the way He lived, then it makes good sense that that is the way we, too, must learn to live."[2]

ACTION ITEMS

✝ *List the things you intentionally do to make rest a part of your life.*

✝ *Whose example are you following when it comes to practicing rest: God's or the devil's?*

Rest is difficult. Not because we disdain the concept in theory, but because the practical consequence of resting involves not working. It is fruitless to consider rest without measuring its impact on work.
—THOMAS ADDINGTON AND STEPHEN GRAVES

Principle Two

Rest is not the opposite of work.

Lettie B. Cowman served many years with her husband, Charles, as a missionary in Japan and China. She helped found the Oriental Missionary Society and became one of the world's most popular writers of devotionals. During her ninety years on earth, she developed a healthy understanding of what she called "the music of rest" in our daily lives.

There is no music in rest, she would point out, but there is the making of music in rest. Thus, rest, or silence, actually is part of the music, not just a stop in the music or the opposite of music.

"Be it ours to learn the tune," she said, "and not be dismayed at the rests."

Biblical rest, according to Stephen Graves and Thomas Addington, authors of *The Fourth Frontier,* is the opposite side of the same coin as biblical work. "Rest and work go together," they say. "It is irrelevant to consider them separately because God always places them side by side. They form a dyad that drives a seven-day rhythm: work six, rest one. Twenty-four consecutive hours out of every 168 must be devoted to rest. God even gave that weekly parenthesis a name—the only day of the week not identified simply by a number. He called it the Sabbath."

Rest is part of life. It is not inaction. It is not laziness.

As Jules Renard put it, "laziness is nothing more than the habit of resting before you get tired." Biblical rest—productive rest—then, is nothing more than resting when it is appropriate.

It can be easy to adapt an antagonistic view of the relationship between work and rest. Work causes things like strain, tension, pressure, and sleepless nights, while rest is the antidote for anything bad caused by work. Or, work produces wealth, success, self-sufficiency, and position, while rest leads to poverty and dependency.

Yet, God invented rest and work at virtually the same time. He meant them to complement, not fight against each other. Each contributes something very different to a balanced, integrated life. Without work, life lacks crucial elements that are impossible to gain any other way besides work. Without rest, we lack what only rest can supply.

If we don't work, we are lazy, we don't provide resources, and we can't fulfill our calling. But if we don't rest, we are shallow, we don't assess direction, and we can't worship our God.

Thus, a godly life is a life of work *and* a life work. Side by side. Working together. Making the music of life.

ACTION ITEMS

✝ *Make a list of the things that create a tug-of-war in your life between work and rest.*

✝ *How can you change your attitudes and your actions so that they both are pulling on the same end of the rope?*

There are so few empty pages in my engagement pad, or empty hours in the day, or empty rooms in my life in which to stand alone and find myself. Too many activities, and people and things. Too many worthy activities, valuable things, and interesting people. For it is not merely the trivial which clutters our lives but the important as well.

—ANNE MORROW LINDBERGH

PRINCIPLE THREE

Work always attempts to invade rest.

The editorial team for *The Life@Work Journal* schedules an all-day off-site retreat every two months to plan the next issue of the publication. And while these meetings are not weighted down with rules, there came a point when the editor had to draw a line in the sand. From now on, he told the team, these will be "gadget-free" retreats: No cell phones, no palm pilots, no laptops, no beepers.

The myth is that technology allows us to save time. The reality is that it allows us to spend more time working—in airports, in our cars, in our homes, on our vacations.

Gordon MacDonald tells the story of how his grandfather traveled by ship to Europe each year as a preacher. "He would spend the five or six days aboard the Queen Mary in a deck chair reading his Bible and praying," says MacDonald. "When he arrived in France, he was ready to go. When I make that trip today in a jet, I spend two days recovering from jet lag. Is there something wrong with this picture?"

There is always some good reason not to rest, because there

always is something else to do. And technology is only part of the problem. "Rest is difficult," MacDonald says, "because, in a knowledge society, we have blurred the line between work and non-work."

If you are reading a book with a red pen or a highlighter in hand just in case you come across a quote or an anecdote that you might pass on to your team or incorporate into a speech, are you resting or working? If you have lunch with a friend and you talk about work, are you working or resting?

There are times, MacDonald says, when he and his wife are taking a trip in the car and she will notice that her husband has grown silent. After ten minutes or so, she inevitably asks if he is mentally writing an article or solving a problem. "I try to convince her that I'm not 'working,'" MacDonald says, "but I know that she knows I'm lying."

Of course, these problems are not unique to our times; they are merely shaped by them. In ancient times, for instance, Nehemiah spent considerable time and effort restoring the wall around Jerusalem, not to mention the laws of God for His people. Then one day he looked out and saw that a variety of commerce was taking place on the Sabbath.

Nehemiah had to draw his own line in the sand.

"When evening shadows fell on the gates of Jerusalem before the Sabbath, I ordered the gates of Jerusalem to be shut and not opened until the Sabbath was over. I stationed some of my own men at the gates so that no load could be brought in on the Sabbath day. Once or twice the merchants and sellers of all kinds of goods spent the night outside Jerusalem. But I warned them and said, 'Why do you spend the night by the wall? If you do this again, I will lay hands on you.' From that time on they no longer came on the Sabbath" (Nehemiah 13:19–21).

ACTION ITEMS

✝ *How is work "invading" the time you need to use for rest and relaxation?*

✝ *How can you alter your schedule or build in checks and balances to protect your rest times?*

We're to live a surrendered life.

—DAN CATHY

PRINCIPLE FOUR

Rest requires faith.

Two brothers grew up in the same home with the same parents, but they developed remarkably different approaches to the concept of rest.

One left little room in his life for anything that did not have an obvious impact—immediate and positive—on his career. His plan was to work at full speed until he reached the age of forty-five, and then, his worldly success secured, he would devote some time to God, family, and leisure. And by the time he reached his late thirties, this brother was well on his way. He owned his own company and was making lots of money.

The other brother worked hard, but he also regularly kept the Sabbath and was committed to spending time with his family. He led a life of pace and balance. His professional career progressed nicely, but not in the manner of his brother's.

This man worried that his success-driven brother would burn out, perhaps even die of a heart attack, before ever making it to his forty-fifth birthday. He had to admit, however, that his brother just might live to be 100. Maybe, just maybe, his brother would have it all—success in the first half of life and time to enjoy it in the second half of life. Maybe he could survive the physical and emotional stress of a nonstop lifestyle. Maybe his wife and children would forgive him for his lack of interest in their lives. Maybe.

While he was not ready to give up his lifelong commitment to balance, he couldn't help but feel a tinge of jealousy. The question of "what if?" hung in the air.

For the independently wealthy, rest is a personal choice. If they do not embrace it, it's mostly likely because they can't overcome a Type-A personality that pushes them to do ever more and more.

For the rest of us, rest is a matter a faith precisely because it will be tested. Short-term measuring sticks almost always demonstrate the value of action over rest, so it takes faith to incorporate rest into our work. There are inherent risks involved with taking time off—the risk that business might suffer, the risk that competition (internally and externally) might pass us by, the risk that our work ethic might be questioned . . .

People who say they have a faith in a higher power can be among the worst at putting that faith into action. Remember the country preacher who gathered his flock to pray for rain during a drought? They arrived eager to pray in faith, but the preacher couldn't help but wonder: Where were their umbrellas?

Faith inherently means putting trust in something other than ourselves for the results that follow an action that on the surface seems illogical. As Charles Spurgeon put it: "A little faith will bring your soul to heaven; a great faith will bring heaven to your soul."

ACTION ITEMS

✢ *How is your faith in the concept of rest showing up in the way you live?*

✢ *Are you taking action and trusting God for the results, or is your faith limited to what you think the world expects?*

I've learned the necessity of stepping back, looking where I was going, and having a monthly quiet day to be drawn up into the mind of God.[3]

—JOHN STOTT

PRINCIPLE FIVE

Rest is a lifestyle (part 1).

Each January, Dan Cathy blocks out two-and-a-half days for Chick-fil-A's annual operators' seminar—that is in addition to the three days when he actually attends the seminar.

As executive vice president of Chick-fil-A, Cathy wants to be at his best—mentally and physically—for the annual seminar, which brings together 1,500 employees for workshops and casting vision. So to prepare, Cathy schedules some intentional down time.

"I don't read my e-mail, and I don't listen to voice mail messages," Cathy says. "I take my books and the Bible and a notepad and some articles, and I read and I study and I think. And I'm able to think deeply about some things."

When David Miller was a director at a large investment bank, he developed a schedule that allowed him to work as late as he needed one night a week while committing to be home by a certain hour the other four nights.

"That really helped both my wife and me," he says. "It gave her dependability, and it gave me rest. It also gave me permission to say no. One concentrated night of working late was hugely productive, as opposed to five nights a week of doing semi-productive work and feeling guilty."

Miller also established the practice of "meetings with myself." He intentionally scheduled fifteen-minute blocks of time three or four times a week when he closed his office door and got away from his desk.

"I realized I needed breathing time during the day so I could create new ideas and not just be in a response mode," he says. "Sometimes I would pray, daydream, or think about a work project."

Miller and Cathy understand that rest does not happen without planning. In fact, for it to have its greatest impact, it has to become a lifestyle. It becomes part of our work life, part of our community life, part of our family life—part of all of our life.

"We've got to be disciplined in the way we manage our schedules so that we can always be at our best," said Cathy. "And we have to be at our best when we get home, too. We've got to have some kind of energy—emotional energy and passion—in the tank to share with our family members, as well."

ACTION ITEMS

✝ *How is rest—or a lack of rest—a part of your lifestyle?*

✝ *How would your family and friends answer that question?*

Busyness is not automatically a synonym for kingdom work. Busyness is only, well, busyness. In fact, busyness is sometimes what happens to us when we forget who God is.

—RICHARD SWENSON

Rest is a lifestyle (part 2).

In an interview with *The Life@Work Journal*, Dr. Richard Swenson, author of *Margin* and *The Overload Syndrome*, listed five suggestions for making rest a lifestyle:

Set boundaries. "Caving in to demands that are emotionally overwhelming, relationally unhealthy, physically exhausting, and spiritually inauthentic is not the way to create the space and rest we all need. This dilemma is best solved by understanding and establishing boundaries."

Protect open spaces. "Don't saturate your schedule. There is no need to feel guilty if your calendar has empty dates and open spaces. On the contrary, it is abnormal and unhealthy to have none. This is the precise message of *Margin*—we need space to heal and time to rest."

Restore the practice of Sabbath rest. "When our culture started to let the Sabbath slip, it was the beginning of a flood of complicated problems. A survey of *Working Mothers* readers showed that 95 percent of people look forward to weekends to rest. But 52 percent were more exhausted at the end of the weekend than they were before. Use the Sabbath both to rest from busyness and to remember God's great deeds on our behalf."

Fast; lie fallow. "Imagine a one- or two-week fast—a total shutdown—from activities. It might be a jarring experience. For most moderns, the experience would be so foreign that we could not tolerate it. For the first few days, we might be so disoriented that we would feel the experiment is not working. As with any withdrawal there might be a nervous feeling, akin to panic. Just because it feels so uncertain is no reason that we should judge prematurely. Remember, it takes time to learn right living, just as it takes time to learn how to ride a bike or detoxify from alcohol."

Free yourself from the opinion of others. "Perhaps the biggest burden we carry is our inordinate concern about the opinion of others. If we could free ourselves from that weighty expectation, we would find ourselves on freedom's road.

"Theologian A. W. Tozer explained it this way in *The Pursuit of God*: 'The heart's fierce effort to protect itself from every slight, to shield its touchy honor from the bad opinion of friend and enemy, will never let the mind have rest. Continue this fight through the years and the burden will become intolerable. Such a burden as this is not necessary to bear. Jesus calls us to His rest, and meekness is His method. The meek man cares not at all who is greater than he, for he has long ago decided that the esteem of the world is not worth the effort.'"[4]

ACTION ITEMS

✝ *On a scale of 1 to 5, with 5 being the best, how do you stack up in regard to Dr. Swenson's prescriptions?*

In the tempestuous ocean of time and toil, there are islands of stillness where man may enter a harbor and reclaim his dignity. The island of the seventh day, the Sabbath, a day of detachment from things, instruments, and practical affairs, as well as of attachment to the spirit.[5]

—ABRAHAM JOSHUA HESCHEL

PRINCIPLE SEVEN

Rest (re)connects us with God.

During the twenty-five years that Chuck Swindoll lived in the Los Angeles area, he and his family occasionally made a ninety-minute drive to a mountain retreat. There, removed from the honking horns, the roaring engines, and the other sounds of the city, they would lean against a ponderosa pine or old oak tree and inevitably comment on the value of stillness.

"Such quiet visits with nature never failed to draw our hearts closer to our God," Swindoll wrote in *Intimacy with the Almighty*. "I can honestly say, such extended visits with silence invariably made us more sensitive to spiritual things, more appreciative of God's presence and grace. In a word, it made us deeper."[6]

There are times when rest might take the form of activity, but anyone who is not experiencing the silence and stillness of rest is missing the deeper spiritual benefits.

"Knowing God deeply and intimately requires such discipline," Swindoll writes. "Silence is indispensable if we hope to add depth to our spiritual life."[7]

Rest, at its best, opens the door for reflection and clears a pathway for communication with God. Throughout Scripture, "rest" means either to cease from work or to reflect on God, depending on the context. In the *Expository Dictionary of Bible Words*, Larry Richards explains it this way: "Each seventh day provided a full-orbed reminder of who God was to His people. He was the source of their life, He was the provider of their freedom, He was the one who ordered their lives and gave them meaning. The Sabbath day provided a rest from the normal activities of life in the world and an opportunity for each believing Israelite to contemplate his roots and his identity."[8]

Likewise, God uses the opportunity to connect with us. As Jesus explained it, "Come to me, all you who are weary and burdened, and I will give you rest. Take my yoke upon you and learn from me, for I am gentle and humble at heart, and you will find rest for your souls. For my yoke is easy and my burden is light" (Matthew 11:28–30).

Because of that invitation, the Sabbath is more than merely laying down work and reflecting on what God has done. It allows us to actually ask for His help in our work. Jesus is offering a lifestyle of rest. He's offering peace. Tranquility. Contentment. Fulfillment. Even if the world crumbles around us, we can take on Christ's yoke and experience the benefits of rest.

ACTION ITEMS

✝ *If you don't already do so, schedule a regular "quiet time" each day for the next week. Use that time to connect with God, specifically as it relates to your work.*

Unlike work, where everything is measured and measurable, rest is not easily gauged.
—TOM ADDINGTON AND STEPHEN GRAVES

PRINCIPLE EIGHT

Rest can be productive personally.

Tom Phillips, president of Raytheon Corporation, was sitting in his office when a longtime friend dropped in for a visit. And at first glance, Tom looked just as he always had looked—jet-black hair, athletic build, no jacket.

But there was something different, something Chuck Colson could not help but notice even if he couldn't quite identify it.

"The smile was a lot warmer, radiant, in fact, and he looked more relaxed than I had ever seen him," Colson writes in his autobiography, *Born Again.* "In the old days, though always genial, he had a harried look—with phones ringing, secretaries running in and out of the office, his desk piled high with paper. Now there was something serene about his office as well as about Tom."[9]

Phillips had discovered the inner peace that comes with faith in Jesus. He had been transformed into something new, something better. And while the old Tom Phillips was not totally gone, there were undeniable changes—positive changes—to his personality. He no longer acted in the same, old ways.

"There was a new compassion in his eyes and a gentleness in his voice," writes Colson.

It is all too easy, of course, to take for granted this gift of rest, even for those who work hard to ground their daily lives in a faith that stresses its importance. In the business of life, the type of rest that Phillips discovered can slowly work its way into the hidden parts of our hearts and minds. It might not totally disappear, but it can be squeezed into a corner so tightly that we miss the benefits that come from a well-rested life.

Gordon MacDonald, the acclaimed pastor and author, has seen how a lack of rest affects his personal productivity, and it is not good.

"I've taken note of the symptoms that suggest that I am not rested, such as irritability, sluggishness of mind, lack of concentration, weariness of spirit, doubt, anxiety, self-pity, a desire to quit," MacDonald says. "Interestingly enough, when I am not well rested, I do not sleep well. My night times are fitful (restless); my mind is clogged and resembles a rush hour of thoughts. In a state of restlessness, I am distant to God, not present to those whom I love the most. Sometimes I make bad decisions, and I lose a certain love for my work. With little rest, my body succumbs to colds and other kinds of illnesses. Life stops being fun."

A life integrated with regular rest, on the other hand, allows us to be our best with our families, with our friends, in our communities, and in our work.

"Those periods of solitude and reflection help shape our priorities and help give fuel to the passion engine that we have inside of us," said Dan Cathy, executive vice president of Chick-fil-A. "If we get flat and don't bring passion to our work, then we best not show our face there until we're ready to bring something to the table."

ACTION ITEMS

✝ *How does rest, or a lack of rest, impact your personality and your personal productivity?*

Somewhere along the line, most of us bought into productivity as a chief value in life. The lie that came along with this value was that the more work, the greater would be the productivity. The end result: rest is dangerous to productivity. We can only rest after the work is done. This is stupid, frankly, but most of us live as if we really believe it.

—GORDON MACDONALD

Principle Nine

Rest can be productive professionally.

When Truett Cathy opened his first restaurant in 1946, he decided that he would close it on Sunday. In part, it was an expression of his faith. He grew up in a family that attended church on Sundays, and he had a deep respect for the Sabbath. But there was a practical reason for closing one day each week. That's because the twenty-four-hour period designated as Sunday was the only time during the week when the Dwarf Grill wasn't open.

"Being closed on Sunday was a relief valve," Cathy said. "I doubt I'd be in existence today if I tried to make it seven days at the pace I was going. We dearly needed the sales. That's why we were open 24 hours a day. But it was a wise decision to close on Sunday."

The success of the Dwarf Grill led to the Chick-fil-A chain of restaurants, and every link in that chain—more than nine hundred stores—shuts down on Sunday. Historically, Sunday trails only Friday and Saturday as the busiest day of the week for restaurants. But Cathy believes that closing on Sunday remains one of the best business decisions the privately held company has ever made.

For starters, it helps attract and keep good employees. Chick-fil-A has one of the lowest turnover rates in the industry, both in management and on the front lines.

"I think they would lose a lot of operators and a lot of respect across the board if they opened [on Sunday] for even a few hours," said Jason Bilotti, who joined Chick-fil-A in 1986 when he was 15 and eventually took charge of a unit in Atlanta. "That's the one day when I'm able to relax. During the week, from 5:30 in the morning until 11:00 at night, I could be called at any time. My wife and I truly enjoy Sunday. You don't get called. You don't deal with the problems."

Regular rest makes for more-productive employees. Dr. Richard Swenson quotes a British survey that showed productivity dropping by 25 percent when people work sixty hours a week. "We might call this another example of the law of diminishing returns," he said.

Sometimes less is more. And if it's not more, maybe it's plenty.

If you ask the folks at Chick-fil-A how much money it costs the company each year not to open on Sundays, they'll just point to their balance sheets. In 1998, for instance, Chick-fil-A's 820 locations generated more than $798 million in sales, and they were on pace to top the $1 billion mark in 2000.

"The world would think that you'd sacrifice 15 to 20 percent of your sales by closing on Sunday, but we don't feel like we sacrifice anything," Cathy said. "We feel we make up the difference. We feel we have been blessed by closing on Sunday. For the most part, we generate the sales in six days that our competitors do in seven days."

ACTION ITEMS

✤ *How has a lack of rest impacted your productivity on the job over the years?*

✤ *Can you point to times when stress and fatigue caused you to make mistakes that you might not have made otherwise?*

The time to relax is when you don't have time for it.[10]

—SYDNEY J. HARRIS

PRINCIPLE TEN

The mind and body need rest.

You won't find it in the Bible, but legend has it that the Apostle John kept a partridge as a pet. The bird was tame, and John often could be found feeding it and tending to its needs.

One day a hunter questioned John about the practical benefit of his hobby.

"Do you always keep your bow bent?" John asked the hunter.

"No," he replied. "To do so would render it useless."

"If you unbend your bow to prevent its being useless," John said, "so do I unbend my mind for the same reason."[11]

The mind and the body require balance. If they don't stay active, muscles turn to flab and mental capacities turn rusty and dull like a knife at the bottom of a creek bed.

Dr. Richard Swenson, a family physician and author of *Margin* and *The Overload Syndrome*, uses the automobile as an analogy.

"If you run it nonstop for 80,000 miles, you burn up the engine," he says. "You can't keep it revved up all the time and expect it to last. In the same way, the body needs downtime—time to rest. Sleep is an undeniable physiologic necessity for every person. Each of us needs time for our body to heal itself when there are abnormalities, like infectious illness. The body is very good at righting itself, but if pushed too hard, the body's self-healing properties are damaged.

"We also have an emotional need for rest. A lot of hormonal and chemical processes that run the body—like adrenaline, for instance—take instructions from the brain. You could say the mind writes prescriptions for the body. The body fills those prescriptions all the time. So when we're anxious or worried, our bodies suffer from the overload of these messages, and we stay driven all the time."

When the body and mind consistently are overworked, it results in what Swenson calls "torque." Compare it to a tire swing on a tree, spun until the rope is tight. Add the weight of stress to it, and the rope likely will break.

"Healthy rest comes when we allow our high degree of torque to completely unwind," Swenson says. "But when torque is at too high a level, it requires an extended period to come down to a restful baseline. Torque isn't easily switched off like a light switch. It only backs off slowly. Many people are wound so tightly they can take months or even years to unwind."

ACTION ITEMS

✝ *Do you get enough consistent rest to truly get "untorqued"?*

✝ *Or do you experience signs of burnout and extreme fatigue within a short period of returning from a vacation?*

✝ *How can you build consistent rest into your schedule to help prevent torque?*

Unexplainable and unexpected events are handed to people in different doses and at different times, but they're bound to happen sooner or later.

—THOMAS ADDINGTON AND STEPHEN GRAVES

PRINCIPLE ELEVEN

*Rest helps us deal with
the stress of change.*

Fatigue is nothing new to the human condition. It is common to all people at all points in history. What is new to our times, to borrow a phrase from Swiss psychiatrist Paul Tournier, is the concept of "universal fatigue." This is a surprising occurrence since it was logical to assume that progress would lead to more rest and more leisure, not less.

What most people failed to factor in was that progress begot change at ever-increasing speeds. The result is that our work might be less physically taxing but it often is much more draining mentally and emotionally.

"People had hard, physical jobs, but such physical activity had laudatory benefits," Dr. Richard Swenson said of the pre-information-based workforce. "Bodies generally are healthier with physical labor. Physical labor actually is good for your brain. The pattern was to work hard with your body and arrive at the end of the day physically exhausted."

Not to mention poor.

Clearly, the vast majority of people in the modern world are far better off economically than people of any previous age. People in the past generally had empty wallets and sore backs. "But they didn't have a lot of stress, because stress, by definition, is related to change," Swenson said. "Things didn't change very much in the past. But the stressors related to change have increased remarkably."

Today, we are worn out by change.

"We feel exhausted, but most of it comes from emotional exhaustion," Swenson says. "You'll notice that when you do something you enjoy, your tiredness slips away. Most of that tiredness and exhaustion is triggered by emotional factors that filter into the body. Muscles themselves aren't tired. It's our minds that are tired."

Rest allows us to deal with change, and thus fight off the mental fatigue that often comes with stress. But it is not just the inactivity of rest that is beneficial. After all, we can do nothing physically and wear ourselves out from thinking about a problem. If we lay awake in bed at 3 A.M. wondering how to meet a client's needs, we are not likely to head to work that day rested and refreshed.

The reason rest helps us with change is not necessarily because we can rest *from* something (our work) but because we can rest *in* something (the sovereignty of God).

"Making something happen leads to high blood pressure, worry, and stress," Thomas Addington and Stephen Graves wrote in an article for *The Life@Work Journal.* "Joining something that God is doing leads to peace, joy, and contentment. In the midst of change, followers of Christ can relax in the knowledge that they serve a God of purpose, order, and love who is willing and able to care for them."

ACTION ITEMS

✞ *How does the fast-paced, ever changing atmosphere impact your ability to rest?*

✞ *How does true rest help you deal with the stresses of those changes?*

Contrary to what many may think, rest is not necessarily synonymous with inactivity. A lazy person or a sluggard can be a very stressed person. To me, rest is a change of pace, a place to get your foot off the accelerator and stop.

—BOB FOSTER SR.

Principle Twelve

Rest takes different forms.

A seven-mile dirt road serves as the "driveway" to Lost Valley Ranch in Colorado, and sometimes the elements—the rain, the wind, the snow—take their toll on it. Potholes form. Erosion creates gullies that lie in waiting for the next passing car or truck.

But it doesn't stay that way for long. And the man smoothing it out with a road grader is likely to be eighty-year-old founder Bob Foster, Sr.

He's resting.

"Sometimes good hard work can be very restful," Foster says. "I come back tired, but rest is not just physical. It's also mental, emotional, and spiritual. I find that just doing something different or out of the ordinary gives me rest."

Dr. Richard Swenson calls it "stress-switching."

"When you really get stuck and frustrated and you can't move any further, the best, most restful thing is to do something completely different," he says. "Go chop wood, for instance, if you usually work at a desk. You may be tempted to lie down, but your brain doesn't get the rest it needs because it keeps working on the problem, the thing that made you stuck."

Of course, no matter the personality type, no matter the degree of hyperactivity in our genes, there are times when we must simply stop to rest completely. But there are other times when rest takes a different form, according to the needs and personalities of the people who seek it.

"Rest is a hard subject to define, because it is defined by different people in different ways," says George Fischer, president of Callaway Gardens resort in southern Georgia. "Some people like to go scuba diving. For some people, relaxation is to go to run a marathon."

For Fischer, a relaxing vacation looks like a seven-day cruise with nothing to do but read a few books and visit with friends and family. It does not look like a trip to Disney World or a fast-paced sightseeing trip to Europe. While those things can be fun, they are not particularly restful.

On the other hand, he knows that some people find a significant form of rest in backpacking or playing tennis or chopping wood or driving a road grader.

"I think we all need to be introspective," he says. "We need to ask ourselves what it is that helps us relax. If you just keep doing the same thing, your body and brain don't have a chance to relax."

ACTION ITEMS

✢ *List some things that you find restful.*

✝ *What activities do you participate in that are significantly different from your work and thus allow you to rest from your work?*

God's companionship does not stop at the door of a jail cell. I don't know whether the sun was shining at that moment. But I know that once again I could see the light.[12]

—MARTIN LUTHER KING JR.
(ON HIS TIME IN A BIRMINGHAM JAIL)

Principle Thirteen

Rest often leads to defining moments.

Diamonds are made under intense pressure, and it has been said that our character is formed and defined by the way we perform in the heat of battle. When we think of the defining moments of great leaders, we usually think of actions they took at critical moments in history.

For Martin Luther King Jr., those moments include a letter written from a jail cell in Birmingham and a speech in which he proclaimed, "I have a dream."

For Abraham Lincoln, they include a bold stand that said all Americans should be free.

For George Washington, they include a boat ride across the Delaware River and a hard, cold winter at Valley Forge.

For Martin Luther, they include a trip to nail ideas for reformation to the door of a church.

For Shadrach, Meshach, and Abednego, three Jews living in exile in ancient Babylon, they include a refusal to worship pagan idols despite the threat of death in a furnace.

Most defining moments, however, are rooted in inaction, not action. The faith and courage to act, in other words, are founded on the prayer and reflection that come from rest.

Martin Luther King Jr. knew that by attending a march in Atlanta he would be arrested, and he was advised not to participate so that he could help raise money for those who did march. To decide his course of action, he spent an hour alone in prayer.

Abraham Lincoln did not wake up one morning, walk into the Oval Office, and suddenly decide that freedom for some was worth the cost of a civil war.

When the snow began to fall, George Washington already had contemplated his commitment to a new republic.

Martin Luther was fully aware of the fire he would light with his challenge to the church.

Shadrach, Meshach, and Abednego didn't wait until the hair on their arms was being singed by fire to decide to follow God at all costs.

And before Jesus began His public ministry, He spent forty days in the wilderness fasting, praying, and reflecting. It prepared him for an onslaught of defining moments, starting with three critical temptations by Satan.

We form our values and decide how we will live during times of rest and reflection.

According to research by Christian Camping International/USA, more than 50 percent of the people in full-time vocational ministry made a "significant spiritual commitment" at a camp or conference center.

It was during a retreat in California, for instance, that Bill

Bright and some friends were inspired to launch a ministry to college students. And it is during moments of solitary prayer and reflection that many business leaders of faith make the critical decisions that define their leadership.

"That is why we are so tenaciously committed to the [idea] that when somebody gets into a different environment, reflective thinking is maximized very quickly," says Bob Kobielush, president of CCI/USA. "And reflection will often lead to substantial life-changing decisions."

ACTION ITEMS

✝ *What life-defining questions or issues are you considering during times of rest and reflection?*

✝ *Do you think more deeply when you have opportunities to rest and reflect?*

✝ *Are you a good steward of that time?*

The office of the Observer *will be closed June 1, 2 and 3 due to good fishing conditions.*[13]
—NOTICE ON PAGE ONE OF THE WEEKLY
NEWSPAPER IN KEWANNA, INDIANA

Principle Fourteen

Environment plays a key role in experiencing rest.

There is something about gardening that draws Trudie Reed closer to God. The turning of the soil. The careful planting of the seeds. The watering. The nurturing. The pruning. The waiting. The watching. The loving.

"I'm a gardener by nature," she says. "At one time I had 100 African violets."

For Reed, president of Philander Smith College, gardening is much more than a hobby. It's part of how she finds rest. And it is part of what makes her good in her work.

"I address my job as a spiritual mission, which means I must have time to reflect on what I'm doing," she says. "Above all, the key for me is listening. To do that, I like to be around plants."

When Reed was tending to her African violets, she was flooded with lessons on life.

"They taught me patience," she says. "I wanted them to bloom, but I had to learn to nurture and fertilize them, to change the soil, keep the right temperature and not water too much. I love to see my plants grow and be healthy; it is really relaxing and peaceful for me."

If she is not finding rest in her garden, she might be finding it while bird-watching. "It takes me out of the everyday tasks long enough to become quiet and to listen and reflect," she says.

Or while strolling along a beach on the Gulf of Mexico. "I pick up shells, listen to the ocean and reflect on my mission," she says. "That's where I really commune with God—around the water."

Or by simply taking a walk around campus. "I realize that my students are the most important reason for me being here," Reed says. "So when I get involved in tasks that drain my energy, I refocus back to my mission and that energizes me. When I get uptight, sometimes just walking around talking to students, getting a hug, hearing about their stories of success or their challenges will give me refreshment."

Cason and Virginia Callaway understood the importance environment plays in attaining rest and reflection. Their dream for such an environment led to the creation of Callaway Gardens, a resort in Southern Georgia.

The resort, which opened in 1952, is best known among golfing enthusiasts as the site of the PGA Tour's Buick Challenge. But while it has golf courses that challenge the physical and mental abilities of the world's best players, the essence of Callaway Gardens is found in the serenity of its landscape.

In addition to tennis courts and sixty-three holes of golf, the resort has thirteen lakes, a horticultural center, a beach, a log cabin, miles of hiking and bicycle trails, a vegetable garden, a butterfly conservatory, and a chapel. Thousands of different plants and trees cover the fourteen thousand-acre property, but its hallmark is the more than seven hundred varieties of azaleas that bloom each spring.

"[Callaway] was looking for a place to relax," says George Fischer, president of the Gardens. "He wanted a place where people could sit and reflect and talk to their God."

ACTION ITEMS

+ *What are the five places where you find the most rest?*

+ *What is it about these locations that allows you to reflect and attain some sense of peace?*

Millions long for immortality who do not know what to do with themselves on a rainy Sunday afternoon.[14]
—Susan Ertz

PRINCIPLE FIFTEEN

Rest can be hard to handle.

For the typical hard-charging New Economy worker, spending a few days at a secluded retreat can renew the spirit and lower the blood pressure.

Ah, the trees. The wildlife. The quiet evenings on the rocking chair. The morning by the creek with a steaming cup of coffee on one side of a lawn chair and a fishing pole on the other.

It's an escape from the real world. No beepers beeping. No fax machine faxing. No computer computing. No cell phone ringing. No palm pilot palm piloting. No . . .

Wait!?! Hang on a minute!

Sure, this might sound like a little slice of heaven, but let's not take it too far. Can we really disconnect from the world? The theory sounds good, but the reality seems like a nightmare—even for the non-type-A personalities.

"We live in a world that demands a type-A personality whether you are one or not," says Bob Kobielush, president of Christian Camping International/USA. "Anybody who is successful these days has had to adapt to a type-A world. Consequently, I find very few people in leadership who don't have a tremendous re-entry problem in a restful or atypical environment."

More than 5.5 million people visit the one-thousand-plus CCI/USA camps and conference centers each year, and about half of them are eighteen or older.

"You almost have to counsel them through the first 20 percent of their stay," Kobielush says. "Once they get the message that this is a place for rest and renewal, those questions just cease. It's an interesting phenomenon."

Despite their focus on disconnecting from the work world and reconnecting with God and His creation, most camps and conference centers have rooms or cabins with private baths and phones; some even have data ports for computers. They recognize the need to mix some work with leisure, so they provide facilities where guests can hook up their computers, reach for a phones, and conduct business.

"When you explain that it's just around the corner and they can come in anytime and use it, there's almost a relief," Kobielush says. "But they have to be intentional about all of those conveniences; otherwise, the retreat experience can be corrupted."

The key for the retreat staff is to manage expectations. There is a fine line between being efficient without appearing rushed (or of taking your time without appearing inefficient).

"The world that we live in is so fast-paced," says Kobielush, "that if they are immediately stuck in an atmosphere that appears too inefficient or too laid-back, it becomes a distraction from the rest you ultimately want them to have when they're with you."

ACTION ITEMS

✝ *How hard is it for you to switch gears and give your mind and body over to rest and reflection?*

✝ *What excuses do you make for not embracing opportunities to experience productive rest?*

God apparently knew that simply defining and mandating rest would not be enough to persuade us to practice it. So He modeled it Himself. He created for six days, then rested for one. Implication: If God actually did rest and did not simply command rest, then who are we to ignore the one-day-in-seven time out?

—THOMAS ADDINGTON AND STEPHEN GRAVES

PRINCIPLE SIXTEEN

Good leaders promote and model rest.

The corporate headquarters for Chick-fil-A has a serene feel to it. Just a few miles from the bustling Atlanta airport, the five-story building is virtually hidden on a large, heavily-wooded piece of property that also is home to hiking trails and a variety of wildlife. And the design of the interior is fresh, with large open spaces, lots of glass, tasteful artwork, and furnishings that are both comfortable and stylish.

But this is a busy place, a place where work happens.

In addition to the corporate staff that run the affairs for a restaurant chain with more than nine hundred outlets, groups of operators and managers from all over the world make regular visits for training seminars.

Typically, executive vice president Dan Cathy often makes his way down to the cafeteria during the lunch hour and visits with whatever group happens to be in town. He eats his meal with them, and then he usually gives a short talk and takes questions. It is a time of encouragement and enlightenment for the employees, a time for Cathy to interact with the troops.

But his leadership duties do not end there.

When the questions end and it is time for him to return to his office and the troops to return to their seminars, Cathy spends a few extra minutes clearing off the tables and taking the trays and plates to the kitchen. "I've got that," he'll say politely to one of the associates as he adds to his stack of dirty dishes.

"We as leaders have to set the standard and model the behavior that we want from others," Cathy says.

That means modeling hard work. When Truett Cathy, Dan's father, opened his first restaurant in 1946, it was open twenty-four-hours a day, six days a week, and there were times when he worked thirty-six hours straight. He and his sons and his other top managers still display a do-what-it-takes work ethic. "When you've got a houseful of customers and you're running out of coleslaw," Truett says, "would it be proper to walk out on a situation like that?" But they also model the principle of Biblical rest.

"That means we have to be at peace with ourselves and keep all these priorities in balance so we'll be able to be creative and so we'll have the energy we need," Dan says. "Otherwise, we get burned out."

Well-rested, refreshed employees do a better job, Dan believes, and it's up to him to provide the model, as well as the policies, those employees need.

"As leaders we have the responsibility of managing the energy that's within our people," Dan says. "Particularly in today's knowledge-based economy, we're really managing innovation and creativity. And innovation and creativity come from a rested mind . . . a mind that's at peace, a mind that's unstressed, a mind that's in balance with other parts of life. Those are the types of creative, excited minds that we need to have surrounding our workplace."

Action Items

✝ *How are you modeling proper rest for the people within your sphere of influence?*

✝ *When they see you at work, are they picking up on stress and panic or peace and restedness?*

ENDNOTES

1. Joshua Heschel, *The Sabbath: Its Meaning for Modern Man,* (New York: Farrar, 1995) 18.

2. Charles R. Swindoll, *Leisure: Having Fun Is Serious Business!* (Portland, Or.: Multnomah Press, 1981), 5.

3. Roy McCloughry, "Basic Stott: Candid Comments on Justice, Gender, and Judgment," *Christianity Today* (8 January 1996): 25.

4. A. W. Tozer, *The Pursuit of God* (Harrisburg, Pa.: Christian Publications, Inc.), 112.

5. Heschel, *The Sabbath,* 29.

6. Charles R. Swindoll, *Intimacy with the Almighty: Encountering Christ in the Secret Places of Your Life* (Nashville, Tn.: Word Publishing, 1996), 43.

7. *Ibid.,* 38.

8. Lawrence O. Richards, *Expository Dictionary of Bible Words* (Grand Rapids, Mi.: Regency Reference Library, Zondervan Publishing House, 1985), 525.

9. Charles W. Colson, *Born Again* (Grand Rapids, Mi.: Fleming H. Revell Co., 1995), 93.

10. Lowell D. Streiker, *Nelson's Big Book of Laughter: Thousands of Smiles from A to Z* (Nashville, Tn.: Thomas Nelson, Inc., 2000), 368.

11. Paul Lee Tan, *Encylopedia of 7,700 Illustrations: Signs of the Times*, Seventh printing (Rockville, Md.: Assurance Publishers, 1984), 1139-40.

12. Martin Luther King Jr., *Why We Can't Wait* (New York, N.Y.: Harper & Row, 1964), 84-85.

13. Tan, *Encylopedia of 7,700 Illustrations: Signs of the Times*, 1140.

14. James S. Hewett ed.; *Illustrations Unlimited*, (Wheaton, Ill.: Tyndale House Publishers Inc., 1988), 478.

More from

Five key areas for integrating your faith into the marketplace

Corporate America is certainly one of the greatest testing grounds for personal faith and conviction. With an increasing number of believers across the globe seeking to integrate their faith into the marketplace, the editors of *Life@Work* have targeted five key areas in work where Christians can apply God's truth—Ethics, Rest, Calling, Ambition, and Coaching. Excellent for individual study or group interaction and discussion.

W WORD PUBLISHING
www.wordpublishing.com

BLENDING BIBLICAL WISDOM AND MARKETPLACE EXCELLENCE

The Life@Work Book

The award-winning *Life@Work* magazine is dedicated to blending biblical wisdom and marketplace excellence. Now, for the first time, *Life@Work* brings together the most intriguing and insightful writings of their contributors in one incredible volume: *The Life@Work Book.* Join Larry Burkett, Laurie Beth Jones, Os Guiness, Charles Swindoll, and other leading Christian writers in the further integration of spiritual life at work.

**The Fourth Frontier
(Stephen Graves & Thomas Addington)**

Unlike other God-ordained institutions—church, family, and government—followers of Christ routinely treat work as a necessity; something we must do to make a living, a separate and disconnected entity of existence. Addington and Graves show that work, in fact, is ordained by God. By exploring such landscapes as calling, devotion, stewardship, influence, integrity, and rest, readers can discover how to have a Kingdom influence in the marketplace while living an integrated life in the Fourth Frontier.

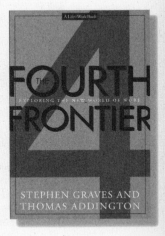

WORD PUBLISHING
www.wordpublishing.com

THE Life@Work Co.

Do you get it?

You can today. For a Free Trial Subscription call 1.877.543.9675 or visit us on the web at www.lifeatwork.com. Act now!

Is there a conflict between your personal faith and your workplace culture? Are you looking for a way to be successful in God's eyes (and not just the world's)? Do you want to build a life of credibility and influence for the Kingdom? Then join The Life@Work Co.® today. In the pages of our magazine you will find men and women who get it — they understand that an integrated life eases the tension between faith and work. They know what it means to be a real success. They are building lives of credibility and influence. And they will show you how.

If you are interested in networking with others who get it. Call and ask about *Life@Work Gatherings* that are meeting in your area. If you would like more information about *Life@Work Gatherings, Life@Work Conferences* or *Life@Work Radio* just call 1.800.739.7863.

Feel free to contact any of the founders via email:

Tom Addington	Steve Graves	Sean Womack
taddington@lifeatwork.com	**sgraves@lifeatwork.com**	**swomack@lifeatwork.com**